Dadgummit

07 08 09 TWP 10 9 8 7 6 5 4 3

ISBN-13: 978-0-7407-5027-4
ISBN-10: 0-7407-5027-5

Library of Congress Control Number: 2004112528

Attention: Schools and Businesses

Andrews McMeel books are available at quantity discounts with bulk purchase for educational, business, or sales promotional use. For information, please write to: Special Sales Department, Andrews McMeel Publishing, LLC, 4520 Main Street, Kansas City, Missouri 64111.

Dadgummit

More Dadisms

CATHY HAMILTON

**Andrews McMeel
Publishing**

Kansas City

Dadgummit

"Keep your eyes on the road."

{ Pity the poor child who learns to drive with Dad riding shotgun, for he or she is to be unwillingly subjected to an endless litany of instruction, the favorite being the above ism. }

The second most popular is *"Brake!"*

"Hands on the wheel at ten and two."

Here's another Driver's Ed rule that dads embrace as the proper and most safe position for new drivers. By grasping the wheel at the ten and two o'clock positions, the driver is balanced, centered, and ready for anything.

(Never mind the fact that Dad's favorite driving position is "Left hand at high noon holding hamburger, right hand clutching cell phone and stick shift.")

"C'mon, Ref! What are ya, blind?"

Most men can't resist heckling the zebras from the comfort and safety of their recliners on a Sunday afternoon. But woe to the referee that dares to make a bad call when Dad is in the stands and his firstborn son, fruit of his loins, has just been fouled on a layup. It is then that Dad will forsake common sense and diplomacy, and question the referee's visual acuity, hand-eye coordination, and, often, intelligence quotient.

At times like this, one can only hope that Mom has the good sense to call a "time out" for Dad in the parking lot.

"Be a good kid and bring your dad a beer, would ya?"

Guaranteed to bring howls of protest from Mom, this request is made when Dad has lowered himself into his favorite chair, remote in hand, and does not intend to move for a very, very long time.

"What a day I had today."

When these are the first words out of Dad's mouth the moment he walks through the front door, it usually means only one thing: "Someone bring me a cold beer before I start to blubber like a baby."

"And pay some schmuck fifty bucks an hour? I'll fix it myself."

All over the world, children have learned to dread these words. Because they mean Dad will be lying on his back under the sink for hours, cussing and barking out commands like "Hold the light steady" and "No, the *other* screwdriver!"

"I remember when a gallon of gas cost $_____." (Fill in the blank.)

Dads have an amazing ability to recall the exact cost of gasoline at any given point in their past, as long as there is a significant historical milestone, usually car related:

"I remember when a **gallon** of gas cost **twenty-three** cents. That was in **1967** when I bought Old Man Thompson's red Mustang, **fixed** it up, and ran Eddie's Camaro into the ground."

"What do I look like, the Power and Light?"

Here's one of the many ways that dads show their contempt for utility companies, especially the electric ones.

TRANSLATION:

"Turn the damn lights off already! I've given those vultures enough of my hard-earned dough."

"Are you ready yet?"

There is nothing more frustrating to a dad than being dressed up in clothes he'd rather not be wearing, ready to go somewhere he'd rather not go, and then having to wait for the rest of the family to leave the house. Maybe it's those itchy dress pants, but dads find it difficult, if not impossible, to simply sit and wait. Instead they pace the halls, monitoring the preparations of everyone else in the household, and pester everyone until they're all in the car.

"Don't bother me unless someone is bleeding to death."

When Dad is otherwise engaged in a very important project like watching the NBA playoffs or stealing a Saturday afternoon nap, his threshold for interruptions decreases threefold. Take the above ism literally. Broken bones, concussions, or knocked-out teeth won't do it. Unless it's profuse, uncontrollable bleeding, don't even go there.

"Now *that's* a car!"

{ Dad's definition of a *real* car: Two leather seats, fire-engine red exterior, convertible top, horsepower out the wazoo, and a knockout blonde riding shotgun. }

In other words, entirely impractical and
existing only in his dreams.

"You've got the whole house. Stay out of my garage!"

Poor Dad. Slowly but surely, he's had to watch while his personal space has been infiltrated by the family. First, he sacrificed his basement to his teenaged son for a black-lit babe lair. Next, Mom commandeered his attic office for a Feng Shui–inspired-crafts-and-out-of-season-decor room. Finally, the den became the "computer room" where kids he doesn't even recognize gather daily to play stupefying war games.

Is it any wonder he's feeling just a bit territorial about his garage?

"Who took my screwdriver*?"

Woe to the kid who borrows a tool and fails to return it to its place on the tool bench or pegboard. For the above question is only Part One of the interrogation. Part Two goes something like this:

"Who told YOU that you could use MY tools? Did you ever think I might **need** that screwdriver someday? Did it ever occur to you to return it to its **rightful** place so that, when that day came, I could find the screwdriver **without** having to tear the whole damn house apart?!"

* Substitute hammer, pliers, wrench, etc.

"I'm going to count to ten, then you better start running."

This statement in no way implies Dad's intent to actually take off running after you. That would be far too humiliating, and Dad's no fool.

This one simply means "Go away."

"There's work to be done and you're out gallivanting around."

Webster's defines "gallivant" as "to roam about in search of amusement or pleasure; to flirt; to run about."

Dad defines "gallivant" as "not mowing the damn lawn."

"Quit your dawdling."

Dawdling (v.): the act of actively doing nothing, as opposed to passively doing nothing (there's a big difference, especially to a teen trying to avoid work). Synonymous with diddling around, dinking around, piddling, and loafing.

Whatever you call it, Dad wants you to cut it out.

"Hardy, har, har."

{ This is a dad's lamest attempt at sarcasm, typically following a child's lame attempt at humiliating him with a comment like "Hey, Dad. Dig those jeans. Expecting a flood?" }

"It's five o'clock somewhere in the world."

When Dad can't wait for the cocktail hour to start, he'll sheepishly offer this rationalization.

"Damn that Uncle Sam."

Usually used in reference to the IRS, on or just prior to April 15.

TRANSLATION:

"Taxes, schmaxes!"

"There are only two things certain in life: death and taxes."

Here's another little gem oft quoted perennially between April 1 and 15. What Dad means here is he'd rather be dead than write yet another check to Uncle Sam.

It is during these times that dads should, if at all possible, be quarantined from the rest of the family and placed on suicide watch.

"Some guys have all the luck."

Typically uttered under Dad's breath upon viewing a portly doofus escorting a beautiful young thing half his age or watching some poor schmuck on TV win an all-expenses-paid trip to fantasy rock 'n' roll camp.

"Don't be a blabbermouth."

Blabbermouth (n.): A person, usually a minor child, who talks too much, especially during the game.

"How 'bout them Yankees?*"

{ This is Dad's all-purpose, one-size-fits-all icebreaker, typically used to start conversation and/or the bonding process with new neighbors, sons-in-law, or first-time dinner guests. }

*Substitute Cubbies, Red Sox, Chiefs, 49ers, or team of Dad's choice.

"I'm all right. It's only a scratch."

Few self-respecting dads will admit to being hurt. Open, gaping wounds or inch-deep punctures generally invoke the above response unless the blood from said wound is saturating Dad's car upholstery. Then, and only then, will a dad become concerned and, sometimes, give in to the notion of applying a bandage to the site.

Dads tend to act stoic when faced with personal bodily injury, but let the damage occur to his personal vehicle and you're likely to hear . . .

"What do you mean 'It's only a scratch'? That's my car you're talking about!"

{ Dads lose all perspective when it comes to their cars. When they notice a scratch or a ding, especially one they themselves did not cause, you're likely to get the same reaction as if they'd just been involved in a three-car pileup on the freeway, as Car No. 2! }

"Don't worry.
It's not a total loss."

It is one of the many ironies of fatherhood that a small car accident triggers a much harsher reaction than a big accident, particularly when a child is involved.

The above ism, uttered as consolation to an inconsolable child, conveys how grateful he is that said child wasn't hurt, even as he's calculating the inevitable hike in his insurance premiums.

"You got your ears lowered!"

This is Dad attempting humor again.

TRANSLATION:

"You got a haircut!"

Sociologists wonder why this ancient colloquialism
has been passed down from one generation of dads
to the next, since it has never been funny,
especially when used with Mom.

"Honey, I'm home!" or "Daddy's home!"

In the old Dick Van Dyke era, a Dad could come through the front door at 5:30, call out the above ism, and expect to be tackled in glee by Mom, 2.5 kids, and Dutch, the slobbering golden retriever. But these days, when Dad gets home from work, odds are the kids are at soccer practice, Mom's still commuting home from her job, and Dutch is out with the dog walker.

"Give 'em an inch, they'll take a mile."

A metaphor that means:

"Give 'em a **piece** of pie, they'll eat **two**."

"Give 'em a $5 **allowance**, they'll take **$10**."

"Give 'em a one o'clock curfew, they'll come **in** at two."

"Give 'em your **heart**, they'll **want** your soul."

"Look me straight in the eye and say that."

Next to the polygraph machine and Mom, a dad is the most accurate lie detector on earth, especially if he can look his subject directly in the eye. Dads say this to ensure they catch every telltale twitch, sideways glance, and eyebrow furl, knowing full well that most kids will buckle under such intense paternal scrutiny.

"I'm getting too old for this."

{ This is what Dad says when, at his children's insistence, he climbs the ladder of the tree house to fetch an errant kite, gets behind the wheel of a bumper car ride, or embarks on a white-water rafting trip. }

"Just try me, Buster!"

{ With this ism, Dad is drawing a line in the sand. Cross that line at your own peril because this guy is primed for battle. }

"You're beating a dead horse now, sister."

TRANSLATION:

"You've asked for a new car six times a day for four consecutive weeks. The answer is still 'No' and if you ask me one more time, I'll see to it that you drive that old Pinto for the rest of your natural life."

"You want some fries with your ketchup?"

This is Dad attempting sarcasm *and* comedy. If you know what's good for you, you'll laugh robustly *and* lighten up on the Heinz.

"God gave you half a brain.
Now use it!"

Now here's a rousing vote of confidence for you. What Dad really means is "Now c'mon. You don't really want my help with that calculus, do you?"

"Let's nip this in the bud right now!"

{ Dads love nipping things in the bud. Some dads could go around bud-nipping all day if there weren't so many other things to do. Among the things most nippable on Dad's list are cussing and other bad behaviors, budding young romance, and a daughter's dreams of becoming a Vegas showgirl. }

"You'll get nothing and like it!"

Mom is out of town on one of her "Girls-Only Weekends." The refrigerator is empty. Dad has scrounged the cupboards to come up with a dinner that could only be described as "Casserole a la Crapshoot." The kids are asking for dessert: "I want ice cream! I want chocolate cake! I want apple pie!" Nine times out of ten, their pleas will be answered with the above ism.

"All the 'sorrys' in the world won't help you now."

When a child is walking the plank toward a punishment so deep and long that he may never see daylight again, he will apologize profusely in a last-ditch effort to achieve amnesty.

This dadism means "Save your breath. It ain't workin'."

"Put some ice on it."

Dad's first line of defense against injuries, cuts, and scrapes is ice. Ice numbs the pain, reduces swelling, and gives Dad a chance to steel himself before examining the disgusting wound at close range.

"Shoulda, woulda, coulda."

By the time most men become fathers, they will have identified approximately five hundred things they should have, would have, or could have done (e.g., earned their master's degree, tried out for the PGA tour, climbed Everest). That's why when they hear a child voicing the same kind of regret, they answer back with the above ism as if to say, "Yeah, yeah. I've heard it all before."

"You better have something to fall back on."

{ This tidbit of sage advice applies to college applications, career choices, and playing Superman on the top bunk bed. }

"Keep your head down."

This is Dad's fix-all for golf problems. It doesn't matter if you've got a hook, a slice, or if you miss the ball altogether, this is the only advice he is capable of doling out.

"Rules are rules."

{ This is Dad's rebuttal when a child makes a good argument against the logic, fairness, or legality of one of the laws he just laid down. }

TRANSLATION:

"I have no comeback at this time,
but I'm not about to let you win this one."

"I can teach you right from wrong but I can't live your life for you."

{ And thank goodness, because if that were the case, your life would be an endless string of lawn mowing, bill paying, yelling at baseball umpires, and car waxing. }

In other words, you wouldn't be having *any* fun at all!

"If I've told you once, I've told you a thousand times . . ."

This is Dad exaggerating. It was probably only a hundred times.

"What goes around comes around."

This is a kinder, gentler way of saying, "You had it coming," which tends not to sit well with a child who has just suffered a sneak snowball payback attack.

"Someday you'll thank me."

TRANSLATION:

"I know you're disgusted right now but, believe me,
in a few years when you've got a place of your own,
you'll be grateful to know how to unclog a toilet."

"Have it your way."

Dad is being sarcastic now. What he means: "Why can't you just admit that my way is better than your way and just save yourself a lot of grief, for crying out loud?"

"Let me tell you a little story . . ."

{ Uh-oh. When Dad opens with this ism, it means you're going to hear one of his special fables, certain to conclude with an appropriate and instructive lesson. }

The moral of the *story* is likely to be no fun at all.

"See what you have to look forward to?"

Spoken with more than a touch of sarcasm, this ism warns against the more mundane of adult chores like cleaning fish, changing diapers, and taking out the trash. If Dad were to be believed, you'd think being a grown-up meant one endless string of stinky tasks.

"Shape up or ship out."

You might hear this one if your dad runs an especially efficient household or served time in the Navy. It is particularly obnoxious when punctuated by the high squeal of a sea captain's whistle.

"You expect me to believe that cock-and-bull story?"

Cock-and-bull story (n.): A tall tale. A lie. An alibi so far-fetched as to be laughable. Commonly used by teenagers caught with cigarettes in their purse ("I was holding them for Jessica so she wouldn't get grounded") or coming home after curfew ("We all decided to go to midnight Mass.")

"Not until you're married!"

TRANSLATION:

"No premarital sex. No premarital cohabitation.
No premarital pregnancies."

And if Dad only has one daughter: No premarital dating!

"I'll have one foot in the grave before I get any respect around here."

TRANSLATION:

"I'm starting to feel like Rodney Dangerfield but without the laughs."

"He can come to the door to pick you up, just like a gentleman should."

Savvy daughters understand that if their dates don't pass muster at Dad's close inspection, they won't get a moment's peace until they do. That's why it's worth it for a guy to suck it up, get out of his car, and call for his date at the door.

"You have no idea how easy you have it."

Nothing drives a dad to distraction faster than a child complaining how difficult his life is. Because what Dad wouldn't give his eyeteeth if all he had to do was study American history, take drum lessons, work on cars, and go to football practice every day?

"Let me introduce you to my better half."

When Dad uses these words to introduce Mom, you can bet he's
   a) trying to impress her friends,
   b) attempting a touch of humor, or
   c) struggling to get out of the doghouse with Mom.

"Boo-hoo.
You're breaking my heart!"

When Dad gets *this* sarcastic, it's best to cease and desist the complaining and just take out the trash, for crying out loud.

"That's the way the cookie crumbles."

The crumbling cookie analogy usually refers to those "You win some, you lose some" scenarios, although it can be applied to Dad's once-a-year baking sessions.

"I'm not getting any younger, you know."

{ Mostly uttered when Dad gets tired of waiting for something, like his turn on the phone, in the bathroom, or at the computer. }

"I'm damned if I do and damned if I don't."

The typical expression of a father's remorse, this ism reflects the frustration embedded in every decision a dad makes in his entire life. It means "Whatever I decide, the kid is still going to complain to his therapist one day that it was all my fault."

"Now *that's* a fire!"

This dadism speaks to man's primal fascination with fire. Dads are enthralled, often even obsessed, with building the perfect fire—be it in the fireplace, campfire ring, or barbecue grill. Each man has his own definition of the perfect fire and, when it is achieved, Dad will step back, admire his handiwork, and make the above proclamation as if he'd just created life itself.

"Out of the frying pan and into the fire."

Another interesting use of the "fire" concept, this ism seems to warn that it's going to get worse before it gets better.

Either that, or Dad's just had an unfortunate cooking accident over an open flame.

"Sometimes you have to go through fire to become steel."

{ Here is the concept of fire used symbolically to represent hard times. Alternately used with "What doesn't kill us, makes us stronger." }

Kids hate this one.

"Where there's smoke there's fire."

Used by dads everywhere, including Smokey the Bear (assuming ol' Smokey has a den of cubs somewhere), this ism is commonly used as a symbolic warning to children to trust your instincts, read the warning signs, and act accordingly.

It's also a good rule of thumb when taken literally, especially if smoke is pouring out the oven door.

"Don't they serve any normal food at this place?"

According to Dad, "normal" food is:

void of any spices except salt and **pepper**.

identified by an easily pronounced **English** name.

served piping hot with "**normal**" condiments (ketchup, mustard, mayo).

eaten with normal **American** utensils (fork, spoon, knife).

priced within **Dad's** budget.

"I'm not talking to hear my own voice."

{ This is Dad articulating his frustration over the fact that nobody in the house seems to be listening to him. }

Kids should never reply with "Huh?"

"What's wrong
with what I'm wearing?"

{ This is Dad being defiant when he steps out in clothing that is less than fashionable, decades out of date, or inappropriate for the occasion at hand. Examples include plaid trousers, velour jogging suits, or Birkenstock sandals with black socks at the beach. }

"These shoes* have plenty of life left in 'em."

Dads have a hard time throwing clothing away, especially if there's an emotional attachment involved. ("Emotional attachment" in this case could mean anything from the jogging shoes worn the first time Dad beat the Johnsons' dachshund to the corner on his morning run to his "#1 Dad" boxer shorts from Father's Day 1997.)

In situations like this, Mom's only recourse is to slip said item into the trash on trash day and claim the house has been burglarized by rag-seeking thugs.

*Substitute jeans, undershirt, boxer shorts, socks.

"I don't care if they're out of style. They're comfortable and I'm wearing them!"

{ Applies to sneakers, old jogging suits, "Alf" T-shirts, coach's shorts—basically any item of clothing old and out-of-date enough to mortify wives and children. }

"Drive or get off the road!"

Dad's definition of **drive**: To move efficiently and unswervingly down the road at all times, preferably at a rate of at least 10 percent over the speed limit, using the appropriate turn signals and obeying all traffic laws, although never to the point of overcautiousness.

If the rest of mankind cannot adhere to this strict interpretation, Dad would prefer they all simply surrender their driver's licenses and take the bus.

"Not in my house, you won't!"

Another way of saying "Not while you're under my roof," this is Dad's way of forbidding behavior that he does not sanction for moral, ethical, or hygienic reasons. Examples include premarital sex, voting Republican (or Democrat), and keeping pet ferrets.

"Who wants gum?!"

Counted among Dad's secret weapons, this ism is used as a diversion tactic when the conversation around him gets too heated, controversial, or intimate.

EXAMPLE:

Daughter: "Well, do you think her problem could be physical?"

Mom: "It could be **hormonal**, I guess. You know her estrogen levels haven't been the same since menopause."

Daughter: "Maybe she should consider using **progesterone** cream or a good sex therapist? I can give her the name of mine, she did wonders for . . ."

Dad: "**Who** wants gum?!"

"Can't a guy get some peace and quiet around here?"

{ **Peace and quiet** (n.): A state of being in which the atmosphere around Dad is void of any discernible sound or movement including screaming children, nagging wives, barking dogs, or Lifetime TV. }

"I'm the chief cook and bottle washer around here."

TRANSLATION:

"As father of the household, I have many important jobs to perform. Some jobs are more important than others. Of course, it doesn't matter. I get just as many complaints from my ungrateful family about the big jobs as I do about the small jobs."

"Stay off of my lawn."

Most of the time, the front and backyards of a home belong to all the people who occupy the household. Kids are free to play on the grass. Mom putters in the garden. Dogs play fetch in the fescue. The exception to this rule occurs during the twenty-four hours after Dad has spent all day in the hot sun mowing, trimming, and/or watering his turf. Then, the lawn becomes his territory and his alone, and woe to the poor creature that dares to set foot on his handiwork.

"I'm a graduate of the School of Hard Knocks."

The School of Hard Knocks boasts an alumni list longer than the entire California university system. Graduation requirements include surviving several doses of rough and unsparing treatment from people or life in general including, but not restricted to, walking five miles to school in the snow uphill both ways.

"Don't make me take off my belt!"

What you *think* Dad means: "Shape up or I'm going to have to deliver some good ol' fashioned discipline, in the vicinity of your rear end!"

WHAT HE REALLY MEANS:

"You'd better shape up because if I really have to take off my belt, these trousers are dropping straight to the floor. And then I'll look really silly spanking your sorry behind."

"Hay is for horses!"

This is Dad's not-so-subtle reminder that, in his unwritten book of etiquette, it is unacceptable to address a person of any stature with the word "Hey!"

Of course, Dad sometimes fails to remember his own rule when he occasionally addresses his own children: "Hey! Stop leaning on my car!"

"You'd better buckle down and get that homework done or it's trade school for you!"

Dads know there's nothing wrong with learning a good trade and, in fact, he may have attended trade school himself. This is just one of many useless examples in Dad's weekly rotation of homework inducers.

It also rarely works.

"I'll give you $10,000 to elope right now."

Far from the knee-jerk reaction you'd assume it is, this offer is the pragmatic dad's way of saying, "I'd do anything to avoid another family meltdown over tea sandwiches, baby's breath, and embossed matches. Just take the money and run. And e-mail us the pictures."

"Don't worry.
I know what I'm doing."

Uttered just before a dad undertakes a daunting task like rewiring a breaker box, capturing a squirrel in the attic, or retrieving a diamond ring from the garbage disposal, this ism strikes fear into the hearts of family members who shudder at the sight of blood.

"You think it's easy?"

Just in case you don't think Dad has it hard enough, here comes this rhetorical question to remind you that nothing, *nothing* in Dad's life comes easy.

"You don't know
the meaning of work."

{ Webster's defines **work** as (n.) physical or mental exertion; labor; employment; one's profession, trade, etc.; or (v.) to cause or to bring about; to make or shape by toil or skill; to cause to be productive; to make or achieve by effort. }

But nobody, not even Webster, knows the real meaning of work except Dad. Because nobody works harder at working hard than he.

"He never did an honest day's work in his life."

TRANSLATION:

"He's a lawyer or a used-car salesman."

"You can do anything you want to, as long as you set your mind to it."

These words of encouragement are used to motivate kids when they are facing scary or seemingly impossible feats such as jumping off the high dive for the first time, going away to sleepover camp, or getting ready to walk down the aisle.

"A man's gotta do what a man's gotta do."

This is what a dad says when he hikes up his trousers, thrusts out his chin, and bolts out the door to prove his manhood by facing something frightening or potentially humiliating.

TRANSLATION:

"Would somebody *please* talk me out of it?"

"How do you *think* it's spelled?"

Along with its handy alternate, "Look it up in the dictionary," this ism is a lot easier for Dad to say than "Are you kidding? I can't begin to spell 'pusillanimous' and I'm too damned old to learn."

"Somebody better confess or I'm getting the strap."

Harkening back to the '50s, when popular parenting wisdom followed the "Spare the rod and spoil the child" principle, this ism is so effective in getting the desired results, it is used by dads who don't even own a strap.

"Trust me."

Spoken with all the sincerity he can muster, this is Dad at his most reassuring. This ism is typically uttered to motivate a child to attempt a challenging, if not frightening, feat like jumping into his arms from the side of a swimming pool, taking a seat next to him on the park's scariest roller coaster ride, or letting Dad take your new car out for a spin.

"What are you, some kind of comedian?"

Sometimes dads are like airport security screeners: They can't take a joke. This is especially true when you make a crack about dad's receding hairline, paunchy waistline, or waning athletic ability. It is at these times when you're most likely to hear the above ism.

Loosely translated, it means "Shut the hell up."

"The door swings both ways."

Don't be confused. Dad is not praising the merits of the two-way door hinge here. This one simply means "If you don't like it, there's the door." (See next entry.)

"If you don't like it, there's the door."

Dads like to introduce the concept of the "door" when they are tiring, for whatever reason, of their children's ungrateful or disrespectful attitude. The "door" becomes a symbol, a metaphor if you will, for access to his good graces, his respect, and, most important, his cash.

"Don't let the door hit you in the rear on your way out."

This is Dad responding to a child's threat to run away from home and never come back. His concern for said child's rear end is sarcastic, at best, because the child has obviously made him extremely angry and he wishes for the child to evacuate the premises immediately.

Ironically, if the door should actually smack the child in the rear as he was leaving, Dad would probably laugh so hard he'd forget what he was so mad about.

"Keep your eye on the prize."

Yet another example of motivational speaking, Dad-style, this ism is used to inspire a child to stay focused on the carrot at the end of the stick. "Prize" in this case could mean a straight-A report card, a paycheck, or an all-expenses paid trip to Disneyland.

"Nervous as a whore in church."

Dads love using spicy little colloquialisms and this one is a popular favorite. Interpreted to mean "*really nervous*," this ism typically causes Mom to shoot Dad "the look" and kids to giggle knowingly.

"It's hot enough to fry an egg on a sidewalk out there."

This ism is one of many that dads use to describe unseasonably hot weather:

"It's **hotter** than blazes!"

"It's **hotter** than a firecracker."

"It's hotter than **Arizona** asphalt."

"It's hotter than the **Mojave** Desert."

"It's hotter than Satan's heels."

Or when it's *really* hot . . .

"It's hot enough to fry an **egg** on my **forehead**."

"Who's the breadwinner around here anyway?"

This ism is Dad's attempt to take back his power by reminding the family of his earning ability. Back in the days of *Leave It to Beaver,* the fathers of the household actually were the breadwinners of the family. These days, when Mom brings home her own paycheck and kids are likely to make $7 an hour at Target, breadwinners abound.

Is it any wonder then that dads think they're losing the fight?

"The damn TV's on the blink again."

On the blink (adj.): Haywire, on the fritz, or inexplicably broken through no fault of Dad's own. Also used in reference to computers, radios, lawn mowers, major and minor appliances and, sometimes, Dad's brain.

"Can't you see I'm busy?"

TRANSLATION:

"Can't you tell, by the intent look on my face and my stiffened posture, that every ounce of my energy is focused on the outcome of this critical third down?"

"Children should be seen and not heard."

{ This is Dad longing for the old days when children spoke only when spoken to and answered questions with "Yes, sir" and "No, ma'am." }

Who is Dad kidding? There were never days like that.

"You're a chip off the old block."

This is Dad giving the ultimate compliment to a son or daughter who has just achieved something of merit like a home run, stellar report card, or a dream job with a salary to match.

TRANSLATION:

"You take after me."

"You're barking up the wrong tree."

{ This is what Dad says when his kids come to him looking for handouts of food, money, or sympathy. }

It's just another way of saying "No"
and Dad has a million of 'em!

"What's the worst thing that can happen?"

This ism neatly sums up the difference between dads and moms. While Mom is making a mental list of everything that could possibly go wrong with, say, a child's first solo road trip (car trouble, tornadoes, murder, mayhem), Dad tends to take the opposite tack.

Moms *really* hate this one.

"I wear the pants in this household!"

Of course, taken literally, this ism is simply not accurate anymore. Everyone in the household wears pants these days. "Pants," in this case, is a symbol representing Dad's manhood, machismo, and presumed dominance over his domain.

Dads can be so deluded sometimes.
Take this one as a cry for help.

"Where do you think you're going?"

This is what Dad says to the child who presumes to leave the house after curfew, during a family gathering, or when there are chores to be done.

TRANSLATION:

"Take me with you, please!"

"Can't it wait till halftime?"

This is Dad's pat during-the-game response to a child's requests like:

"Dad, I have to go potty!"

"Dad, there's a wasp in my room!"

"Dad, Jason stepped on a nail!"

"Dad, something's wrong with Fluffy!"

"Dad, Mom called. She's waiting for you at the airport!"

"Fuhgettaboutit!"

This is Dad doing his best Tony Soprano imitation. It could mean one of two things: "Don't worry about it" or "Don't even go there."

But, chances are, Dad just enjoys saying it to practice his Italian accent.

"You're killin' me!"

TRANSLATION:

"Your repeated arguments and/or bad behavior are manifesting in me such physical symptoms as high blood pressure, heart palpitations, heartburn, insomnia, headaches, and sexual dysfunction. And just once, I wish I could make you feel guilty about it!"

"Suck it up."

Alternately used with "Shake it off," this is Dad's all-purpose remedy for injuries to the body, heart, or ego such as blows to the gut, stinging insults from the opposite sex, or not making the varsity team.

"Why the long face?"

{
If there's one thing a dad can't stand, it's seeing his
offspring pouting or down in the dumps. This is what
Dad says to open a dialogue when he's sure he's not
the reason for the kid's sad sack.
}

"Make yourself scarce."

Used alternately with "Make like a tree and leave" and "Go out and play in traffic."

TRANSLATION:

"Leave the immediate vicinity. Immediately!"

"If you play your cards right, I might let you out by Christmas."

{ When Dad makes this statement as he's closing the door to your room, with you inside, you might as well settle in for the long haul. He's mad and he's not going to take it anymore. }

"You gotta get out there and pound the pavement."

Pound the pavement (v): to endeavor, without procrastination or time off for lunch breaks, to find a job, no matter how menial, laborious, or low-paying, if only to get Dad off your back.

"Pick a number from one to ten."

Solomon not withstanding, Dads are king when settling arguments between their offspring. The above example is one of the more common tactics used to arrive at all-important decisions like who gets to go first on the swing or who gets the biggest piece of cake.

Other proven methods include choosing straws, flipping a coin, and the timeless classic, "Eenie meanie, minie mo."

"Stop contemplating your navel and get to work."

There is no recorded proof that a child ever was caught in the act of actually contemplating his or her navel, but that doesn't stop Dad from making the accusation. Nothing bugs Dad more than a kid avoiding work. And nothing will stop Dad from contemplating it.

"It's only money."

This ism can serve two distinct purposes:

1. **Console** a child who has lost or foolishly spent his hard-earned **cash.**

2. Rationalize Dad's own **misfortune** at the track, casino, or **poker** night.

"That's okay.
You'll get 'em next time."

This is what Dad says when, despite his fervent cheers from the bleachers ("Go, fight, win!" "Kill 'em!" "Mop the floor with those wussies!") his child's team ends up on the short side of the scoreboard.

This ism is typically followed by "Who wants ice cream?!"

"I'm gonna get out of these wet clothes and into a dry martini."

This is Dad's clever way of saying, "That was the most miserable fifth grade soccer game I've ever witnessed in a downpour. I don't care if it is two in the afternoon, I'm having a drink."

"Who the hell
do you think you are?"

{ This is what Dad says when one of his children makes the grave mistake of attempting to call the shots on Dad's turf. }

TRANSLATION:

"Give me a break, will you? I've got little enough
clout around here as it is!"

"Clean up your act."

This all-purpose ism has many possible translations: "Stop cussing." "Bring up your grades." "Pick up your room." "Get a job." "Put some clothes on." "Shape up or ship out." "For crying out loud, when's the last time you had a shower?"

"You're getting too big for your britches."

This is Dad giving you fair warning that you're about to receive a comeuppance. His objective is to bring your inflated ego down a notch or two. He'll tell you it's for your own good but he's really going to get his own perverse pleasure from it.

There's little else to do but sit there and take it.

"Who's your daddy?"

This is what Dad says when he's just over-delivered on his paternal obligation with something intensely coveted by his family, such as impossible-to-get concert tickets, a trip to Disney World, or a new car.

"You're spending money like a drunken sailor."

{ Unless Dad happens to *be* a drunken sailor, he will typically use this ism as negative commentary on a family member's reckless squandering of his or her "good money." }

Nobody knows why dads use the expression
"good money" since all money is "good money"
in a dad's eyes.

"You've got to fight the good fight."

{ Dad defines "the good fight" as an honest and determined effort to succeed in whatever one is trying to achieve. }

As opposed to the "bad fight," which means a fight you can't win . . . like the ones he has with Mom.

"You're the most beautiful girl in the place."

Dads tend to be more than a little prejudiced when it comes to their daughters. You can be stricken with the world's worst case of acne, sporting the most horrific haircut of your life, and stuffed into last year's dress that's two sizes too small, and you'll still hear these words of praise from Dad.

"I love you, kid."

{ No translation necessary. }